Supply Chain Management

By

Khalid Zidan

Table of Contents

The information herein is offered for informational purposes solely and is universal as so. The presentation of the information is without a contract or any guarantee assurance.

The trademarks that are used are without any consent, and the publication of the trademark is without permission or backing by the trademark owner. All trademarks and brands within this book are for clarifying purposes only and are owned by the owners themselves, not affiliated with this document.

Introduction

The supply chain is not a new concept for economists. The idea of the supply chain is a basic one that has permeated economic systems since the earliest days of trade and commerce. It is simply a term referring to the collection of businesses or individuals responsible for transforming raw materials into products and then getting those products into the hands of consumers. Though it may be obvious to some, it is important to remember that supply chains exist whether or not they are managed—it is a term that refers to the processes necessary to turn raw materials into a product and distribute them to customers.

The difference in the modern era is not that supply chains have been invented but that they have become a much more complicated proposition, given the expansion of the international economy that's been made possible by the rise of the internet and globalization. Whereas in the past businesses worked with mainly local or regional suppliers and factories, the door is now opened for a company in the United States to own a factory in India and a warehouse in Japan—all without having ever stepped foot outside their city. The customer end of the supply chain has been similarly opened up. Shopping on the internet allows anyone, anywhere to find and buy from your company—a double-edged sword that lets you expand your reach even as a small business but also increases the competition presented by other small businesses everywhere in the world.

Effective supply chain management involves a thorough—and current—knowledge of your industry. Analyzing market trends and correctly forecasting the potential changes in sales in the upcoming season is necessary to stay on top of changes in your business that could affect your bottom line down the road; communicating those potential changes to the rest of the supply chain—both upstream and downstream—is imperative if you want to get the maximum possible profit margin while still maintaining product quality and presenting a legitimate value proposition to your customers.

The information outlined in the following chapters applies to all manner of businesses, from the smallest mom and pop operation to a Fortune 500 multinational corporation. Regardless of size, the premise is the same: raw materials are mined and processed into consumer goods, which are delivered to customers through some means of distribution. As is so often the case in life, the devil is in the details. The details included in this book are an overview of supply chains that can be applied to all manner of industries and management systems and, ultimately, will give you a better understanding of the immense complexity of effective supply chain management.

Chapter 1:
Introduction to Supply Chains

At its most basic level, a supply chain is the series of steps and businesses required to create a product and put it in the hands of a consumer. It encompasses every level of the process, from the mining of the raw materials to product development and production, through the transportation of that finished product to stores and the way it is delivered to the consumer's home. Included in this chain is a broad range of companies and individuals handling a wide array of resources and information.

The supply chain has always existed in economies, but it was only with the expansion of globalization that the inter-connectedness of various steps along the chain could be truly appreciated and explored in depth. Globalization is nothing new, either; even the modern application of it started with container shipping in the 1950s, a full 40 years before the advent of the internet. The idea of controlling the extended enterprise, however—the network of businesses that collaborates to provide a final product—only became a matter of interest for economists in the late 20th century.

There are four broad sections within every supply chain. The first is the cultivation, management, and regulation of natural resources. The exact types of people involved in this step of the supply chain often depend on the nature of the resource being discussed. In the case of cultivated resources, farmers will have a significant role; in the event of mineral resources or wild-grown plants, biological, ecological, and regulatory boards are more likely to be the primary factor.

The second broad section is the extraction or collection of resources and raw material, including the transportation of those materials to the factories or manufacturing plants where they'll be processed. Labor cost is more likely to play a role in pricing at this stage of the chain, and ecological regulations are still likely to be a factor, especially when it comes to mining and drilling for minerals.

The third stage of the supply chain is the one people most often consider when they think of supply chains, and that is the production of raw materials into consumer goods. Depending on the product, this stage could take place within the confines of a single factory or may undergo multiple stops along the way. For a complex machine like a car, for example, the individual components of the machine must first be produced in their factories before being transported to another location for assembly. There may also be third-party distributors of parts and components involved, or warehouses and storage facilities.

The final stage is the distribution of the finished product to the consumer. This step also includes the transportation of the finished product from the factory and often its storage in a variety of warehouses, whether those are owned by the company that produced the product or the one distributing it. The size of the market is going to be the biggest determining factor in how many steps exist at this stage of the process. A company shipping internationally will invariably have more levels at this stage of the supply chain than one distributing locally. The nature of the product will have an impact on this stage, as well. Some products, notably perishable items, may require specialized storage and distribution centers. There may also be an element of government regulation and international relations in this stage, especially for controlled products, such as pharmaceuticals or firearms.

The company or individual that develops the product (or service, as the case may be) is known as the original supplier. The final consumer of the product or service is referred to as the customer, but there are many transactions that occur between individuals or companies along the steps of the supply chain. Each of these businesses or individuals is seeking the maximum possible profit for their stage in the process, meaning that, at each stage, there are negotiations that impact both the final price and the form of the end product. Decisions of cost versus quality arise at every link in the chain, and individuals at one stage may have no knowledge of or interest in the remainder of the production process. A factory that produces steel will see its product being used in a variety of applications; their interests may not necessarily align with those of the car industry, or the appliance industry, or with the consumers who ultimately use the products made from their metal. Because of this, an optimal balance of cost and quality requires someone who sees and analyzes every link in the chain. This long view approach is known as supply chain management.

Development of SCM

Supply chain management (or SCM) first gained traction as a term during the 1980s, when companies began to see the need for a universal view of the various transactions involved in the production and distribution of a product. The ultimate goal of this vertical integration of business processes is to provide goods and services that fulfill the customer's needs as efficiently as possible, with a minimum of waste and the lowest possible inventory.

The main idea behind SCM is to open communication between the industries. Sharing knowledge about fluctuations in market prices and transportation times or costs. This cross-level communication also has an impact on product designs, allowing improvements and developments to the overall quality of the product to be exchanged between otherwise different companies. A retail store might know more about what the customer is looking for in the product and can share this information with the factories, which in turn communicate with their suppliers of raw material as well as research and development departments to come up with the most appealing product from the customer's perspective, ultimately improving sales. Tracking and analyzing sales across regions allow companies to distribute inventory properly and limit the need for warehouse and storage space or the waste caused by a supply that exceeds demand.

The idea of supply chain management effectively changed the global market once it took hold. What was once a competition of company versus company was now greatly influenced by the effectiveness of each company's supply chain. The varied influences on the outcome of a sale, once recognized and analyzed, could be altered and optimized; the company that utilizes its supply chain most efficiently and more is, in the global market, often the most profitable.

The omnichannel supply chain

With the rise of the internet, both companies and consumers now have access to a wider range of products, services, and information than were available in the past. A customer in New York City can buy a product from a store in Tokyo at the click of a button. This metaphorical shrinking of the world has changed the nature of competition in many industries. On the one hand, it significantly expands the potential reach and customer base of any given company; on the other, it means you are competing not only with similar businesses in your region but perhaps even those around the world. The need to create a product that will attract the consumer's eye is more important than ever. The prevalence of online reviews and word of mouth accounts through social media has also made it more important than ever for companies to provide excellent customer service and to be responsive to the needs of their clients. An awareness of the social, economic, and environmental implications of the production process is also often expected from companies in the modern world.

In an omnichannel supply chain, one central pool of stock is delivered to customers through multiple retail channels. This can include brick and mortar franchises, mail catalogs, online stores, and mobile apps. The central stock pool dictates the price of items across retail channels and is also responsible for fulfilling orders and arranging distribution. This model allows companies to cater to a customer base with increasingly more demanding expectations for convenience. Managing the stock across multiple retail channels can be far more complicated than the business model of a single store and many companies take advantage of third party services with experience managing omnichannel supply chains.

Along with the new logistical issues companies face in the internet era, the design of products is expected to be more dynamic and responsive to customer opinion than it has been in the past. Rather than solely developing products that meet existing demand, many companies now develop products that generate demand, fulfilling a new need or introducing a new feature that will bring customers to the brand. These changes to the product design may mean new links in the supply chain. As with the distribution demands of an omnichannel supply chain, this can be far more complicated than the old model in which the product was static, feedback from customers was not as prevalent or accessible, and companies relied solely on marketing for customer generation.

While it is possible than ever before in history to conduct business easily across the planet, it is also more important than ever for businesses to consider the costs and logistics of transportation when conducting global business. Not only do the costs of materials in various areas of the world often fluctuate over time, but the cost of freight and shipping of that material can also change, as well. The savvy logistical mind can find the ultimate balance between product cost and shipping expenses.

Ethical considerations

Consumers in the modern era are both more aware of and more concerned with the ethical treatment of workers, not only in the factories owned by major companies but throughout their supply chain. Now that businesses have the option of working with various suppliers and factories at earlier stages of the supply chain, it is seen as part of their responsibility to ensure that those suppliers they choose to work with are conducting themselves in a positive and ethical way in their businesses.

A lack of transparency within the supply chain is known as mystification. This prevents consumers from being able to find out where the materials and factories used for their end product come from, making it possible to defy the ethical guidelines of the culture or even regulatory bodies unscathed.

As the internet continues to make more information available to consumers, they are more likely to object to socially irresponsible business practices they learn about in the businesses they support, and more likely to ultimately discover the underlying ethical issues that unsavory companies attempt to hide through mystification.

The global trend is for companies to design and integrate ethical guidelines into their corporate cultures and then enforce those guidelines on any companies they work with at earlier links of the supply chain. This is often focused on correct business practices regarding worker's rights and working conditions, but may also enforce environmental regulations on pollution and other natural impacts. Questions of a company's responsibility to uphold their ethical standards in the other businesses along the supply chain—both domestic and international—are a hot-button issue that's often polarizing for both business owners and consumers, who often must make the decision between enforcing ethical business practices and maintaining the lowest possible price on products.

Supply chain optimization

There are many ways that the supply chain can be optimized to provide the smoothest, most efficient production process from start to finish. Communication with suppliers can limit or eliminate bottlenecks in the production process, making products available more consistently and without delays. Materials can be sourced to get the right balance of low material cost and affordable transportation cost while the right factory and warehouse locations can provide a supply only where the market has a demand. Logistical analysis of the company's shipping area can help better to route freight shipments for the most efficient transportation of goods, or determine where new distribution centers should be situated—or which existing ones can be retired. Dynamic logistics that respond to real-world and real-time factors and can adapt to changing situations are the most effective in this modern era of optimized supply chains.

A well-optimized supply chain is also able to cope with and adapt to change, another important feature in today's fast-changing world. There are four basic areas at play in a resilient supply chain. Management has to be reactive, changing tactics and areas of emphasis along with the shifting market. The internal supply chain should be well-integrated so that products move seamlessly from one stage of the process to the next. This often involves some collaboration across links in the supply chain that may not have communicated with each other under old models. While cooperation is important, however, there should be sufficient buffers in place so that a failure or issue on one link of the supply chain does not have a chance to impact the rest of the process greatly. Finally, the well-optimized supply chain is dynamic and flexible, able to adjust to and recover from shifts in the market or availability of raw materials.

In some ways, the ability to cope with change is the next logical step in the evolution of international business. It was the ultimate goal since the idea of the supply chain was first introduced in the mid-twentieth century: to make the process of developing products and delivering them to customers both efficient and adaptive, so that the business can deliver the best product at the lowest price regardless of other market conditions. As the far-reaching effects of globalization become known, it is more important than ever to have a well-optimized and resilient supply chain if a business hopes to compete in that world market.

Chapter 2:
Supply Chain Modeling Past and Present

The basic idea of the supply chain has remained the same since before the business world put a term to it: maximum profit from minimum inventory. How that goal is achieved, however—and the ease with which companies can reach that goal—has changed significantly since the idea of the supply chain was first introduced.

Globalization and the rise of the internet age are the primary factors at play when it comes to changes in the supply chain between the historical and the modern eras. The ease of communication across wide distances in the modern era has expanded and altered the landscape. It is also both more possible and more important than ever before in history for a business to have a dialogue with their customers. More so than before, demand in the modern era is directly customer driven—not simply in the abstract idea of supply and demand, but in the individual customer's ability to give their input to a company, and their expectations that this input will be heard and appreciated. Responsive product design and distribution are key to the modern supply chain model for a business to be truly competitive in the global marketplace.

There is some traditional way of thinking about business that is outdated in the modern world. First, the management of the supply chain is of paramount importance in the modern era. Where in the past many businesses could get away with paying minimal attention to the efficiency of their supply chain—especially in the food and consumer goods industries—the level of competition in today's marketplace demands attention to these aspects of the process. The efficiency of distribution and supplier networks should be among the top priorities of any modern business.

Secondly, the concept of marketing is entirely different in this customer-driven era. The concept of regional advertising—which is designed to have mass appeal and then broadcast over broad distribution networks, like TV spots, radio ads, and mailed advertisements—is no longer applicable to most businesses. While this still can have a role in the overall business structure, personalized advertisements directed through social media are often far more effective. Though marketing may seem somewhat separate from the supply chain, as with many complex systems it is all inter-related. Regional marketing meant businesses could anticipate a spike in demand in certain areas where their advertisements had been run. Personalized marketing through social media or other online venues could bring in business from anywhere in the world, meaning the supply chain needs to be fully optimized and able to meet rising demand wherever it should happen.

The most important of the ways the concept of the supply chain has changed in the modern day, though, is that it can no longer be thought of as a one-way road. In previous conceptions of the supply chain, each step along the chain had only one direction of influence. The raw materials went to the factories; the products went to the warehouses or retail outlets, the warehouses distributed products to the consumer. No link along the chain, in this idea of things, could influence what had come before it in the chain. This is no longer the case. In the modern optimized supply chain, communication can be seen more as a network than a road. Customer feedback can influence the distribution of the product, the design of it, even the raw materials used in its production and the locations they are sourced from. This kind of responsive and dynamic supply chain allows modern businesses to compete in the current global landscape, where there are seemingly endless options available to the modern consumer.

Replacing these old, outdated ways of thinking are some new rules and ideas on how to run a successful business. The importance of reputation in the modern marketplace cannot be overstated. Consumers want to work with companies that are honest and open about their identity and consistent in their practice of business ethics. A company has to know where their raw materials and products are coming from and has to pay attention to whether materials are harvested and goods produced in a way that's environmentally and socially responsible. Certainly, as a business, you do not want your customers knowing more about the details of your supply chain than you do, and the information age has created a consumer class that's better informed than ever before in history.

The expansion of the potential customer base also means an increase in the importance of efficient warehouse and chain distribution to minimize waste. In the old model of business, where many companies worked more regionally, maintaining massive warehouses full of product in a few key locations enabled companies to meet demand promptly. This is not a functional model when your distribution range is global; maintaining a warehouse in every area where you might have customers would mean an incredible amount of inventory sitting unused for long periods of time. To cope with this shift, companies must take a dynamic approach to shipping and distribution, one that often utilizes the talents of a third party service.

A modern approach to supply chain management also incorporates some post-sale support. In older business models, it was acceptable for post-sale support to happen largely at the retail and distribution stage; a company focused only on the production of the product was not necessarily expected to make any contribution to the process once the finished product had been delivered to the store. This has also changed in the information age. Customers now expect a guarantee of quality that includes refund or replacement of the product should they feel it is not up to their standards. This makes the efficiency of distribution even more important.

Some models have been developed to help businesses better understand and navigate the complexities of the modern supply chain. Some are very general and can be applied to almost any type of business while others are more industry-specific. Using a model to manage your supply chain can help to make sure you are not ignoring any links of the chain and can be an incredible asset in staying up to date on changes and issues at all stages of the production and distribution process. Choosing the right supply chain model for the product is a key first step in maximizing the chain's overall efficiency.

There is no single supply chain model that works best for every type of business. The specifics of your product or service will dictate which model works best for you to a certain extent, but the truth is different models excel at different things, and what you hope to improve your business by using a supply chain model will have perhaps the largest influence on which type of model is right for your business.

Modeling for efficiency

Businesses in highly competitive industries often benefit the most from a supply chain model aimed at maximum efficiency. This is especially true of products that are more practical in nature, where many customers are more likely to make their decision based on price than brand loyalty or product features. These products also tend to have relatively consistent sales across seasons with fewer noticeable peaks, making it logical and cost-effective to maintain a running stock continuously, with potentially larger production runs based on long-term sales expectations.

A model aimed at pure efficiency is going to be the most like traditional supply chain models and the least affected by globalization. Under this model, it is often worth the investment to maintain a larger warehouse and back stock of inventory in regional centers to ensure that customers can receive their product promptly, even at peak times. The production sequence will often be fixed, with the goal of producing as much of a single product as possible in one run to reduce the time wasted for set-up and changeovers. Though the managers should keep abreast of major fluctuations in relevant markets, the management strategy overall will be less reactive and more predictive. In this model, managers are often best served by analyzing recent trends, current inventory, and past years' performance to determine the best product runs. The accuracy of the manager's forecast will have a significant impact on the supply chain's overall efficiency.

Modeling for flexibility

In industries where demand can fluctuate widely and unpredictably, a supply chain model that emphasizes flexibility will often be the most effective. Companies working on these models can adapt their internal processes to the level of demand, and it is a far more common model among service companies than those which provide material goods. The ultimate goal of these models is to provide the customer with the ideal balance of quick response and personalized service; customers are often willing to pay more for excellence in these categories.

Managers of flexible supply chains tend to focus on efficiency in the order and delivery process so that it can be navigated effortlessly when demand increases. The ability to marshal extra resources at critical times—sometimes even by collaboration with competitors—can also be key in meeting sudden influxes of demand. Communication with suppliers of resources is also critical. Given that customers are often willing to pay extra for quick and dependable service, higher cost on-demand style relationships with suppliers may ultimately be the best strategy in critical times.

Modeling for on-demand production

While customization can be a factor in many different industries, there are certain instances in which each product is made to such exact specifications from the customer that the production cannot begin until after the order is placed. This model of supply chain eliminates the need for warehouse or storage facilities to house excess product, but should maintain larger inventories of the materials and individual components that go into making the product ensure they'll be available when an order comes in. The emphasis on this model is on the speed and capabilities of the production line to be able to meet demand without significant customer delays.

Managers of this model of the supply chain will face the greatest challenges in the area of production capacity. Accurate forecasting of demand and market trends is important in maintaining short delivery times to the customer. A production model that allows partial completion of products before the stage of customization will streamline the process, and while it is not always possible, managers should consider ways to increase batch sizes whenever possible to minimize their costs per item.

Modeling for speed

Products with a short lifecycle that are seasonal, topical, or otherwise trendy will be best served by a supply chain model that emphasizes speed in the production and distribution, even if it is occasionally at the cost of some efficiency or quality. The customer of these industries is by and large most concerned with the company's ability to adapt to a changing market and provide products aligned with (or even in advance of) current trends. Companies in the apparel and fashion industries, especially those that sell primarily through catalogues, are an excellent example of an industry that would be best served by a speed-based supply chain model.

Smaller production runs are often in order in this type of model, as an excess of stock at the end of the season is unlikely to recoup costs. Products may undergo only one or two production runs depending on the length of the industry's season. Manager focus should be on keeping the company constantly up to date with current customer demand and on reducing the time it takes to get a product from development to market. Though forecast accuracy is important in all supply chain models, it is especially critical in a model built for speed.

The anticipation of market trends can make or break a selling season.

Modeling for stability

In industries that don't rely on seasonal business and have a relatively consistent customer demand profile, it may be best to utilize a supply chain model that supports a continuous flow of products to the consumer. In this model, companies often have a set amount of stock that they make available to customers at all times, with production runs designed to refill this stock up to a set par, either as needed or on a pre-determined schedule. It may also be an effective model for products with short shelf lives, like perishable foods; in this case, production and delivery will occur on set days, their numbers often based on estimated demand with minimal excess inventory.

Businesses are most effective under this model when they use a scheduled order cycle—with orders placed and fulfilled on pre-determined days—rather than a lead-time cycle. This helps to prevent peaks in the demand that could wipe out portions of stock and disrupt the flow of product. Because these types of businesses are more likely to be working in the long-term with both suppliers and customers, it tends to be the most collaborative of the models. Customers may communicate not only their responses to the products but may be expected to discuss variations in their order patterns ahead of time, especially if demand will be significantly changing. The manager's responsibility in this model will be primarily in communicating with customers and suppliers to maintain the steady flow of product at all levels. Close monitoring of sales and inventory information is also especially important to avoid either waste or interruption to product flow.

Chapter 3:
Upstream Processes

The analogy of a river is often used to explain the supply chain. Imagine the raw materials as the source of the river, and the ultimate customer as its mouth. In the simplest possible business model, the raw materials are the product, and they are sent downstream to the customer with no other stops along the way. This still happens in some areas of the modern business landscape—a prime example would be a customer who buys fresh produce directly from the farmer at a farmer's market. In this situation, there is a one to one exchange. The product goes downstream to the customer while the money goes upstream to the farm.

In most situations, though, the customer is not buying raw materials but instead the products made from those materials. When this is the case, the business in question is not located at the mouth of the river but somewhere along its length. Those products, once manufactured, will be sent further down the river to the customer; for the raw materials, though, the business has to turn its attention the other way, too, going back up the river to get the materials it needs to make its finished product.

Generally speaking, upstream in supply chains refers to the first two broad sections of the supply chain mentioned in chapter 1: the development of natural resources and their extraction from the earth. Note that the processing of these resources is not mentioned here; manufacturing, even if it is a component that will ultimately become part of something else, is considered part of the downstream side of the supply chain.

Though need and customer demand may somewhat dictate the rate of resource extraction, generally speaking, the upstream steps in the supply chain are influenced more by the availability of resources than they are by fluctuations in customer demand. This has the potential to make upstream processes more stable than those on the downstream side, but it can also mean that upstream processes are a limiting factor in the ability of a company to meet customer demands if only so much of the raw material can be produced or extracted. Increases in demand which exceed the production capabilities of your suppliers may necessitate the addition of new suppliers or even a shift in the types of materials that are used in the finished product.

The same company may handle the management and extraction of resources, or they may be two separate steps in your supply chain, depending on what industry you are in and what resources you are dealing with. Fluctuations in pricing on the upstream side also differ from those on the downstream side because they are less based on customer demand and more based on resource availability. On the flip side of that, changes in the cost of raw materials are likely to affect all companies within a given industry that utilizes those products. Ultimately, this means that though there is less that can be done from a supply chain management perspective to lower costs and increase profits on the upstream side, these cost fluctuations are also less likely to have an impact on a business' ability to be competitive in the global market for the industry.

The upstream side of the supply chain is important for goods-based industries more so than it is for those that offer services. Industries that are especially concerned with the upstream side of the supply chain include the energy industry (both petroleum-based and alternative sources), biotechnology companies, pharmaceutical companies, and those dealing with metals and minerals. It can take the form of naturally occurring or cultivated resources; the controlling factors and challenges involved will obviously be different depending on whether the resource can be created in greater quantities to suit demand. As mentioned in the first chapter, government regulations of land and resources are likely to play more of a role in upstream processes than it does on the downstream side of the supply chain.

Natural resource management

Raw materials can be loosely defined as any item that is mined or harvested directly from the earth, rather than being produced in a factory. The management of natural resources has increasingly become the focus of government agencies and international politics as concerns continue to grow around the consumption of resources outpacing the ability of the earth to produce them. The term "stewardship" has become a major concept in the management of natural resources. Stewardship represents the idea of controlling the use of resources so that they will not be depleted and will remain available to future generations; government regulations often have more of an impact on the stewardship of resources than do the actions of particular companies or individuals.

Natural resource management puts a focus on understanding the impact of raw material development on the overall ecology of a region. Environmental concerns have become especially topical in the lumber, metal, and petroleum industries, but also have an impact on farmed resources. The emphasis in the present day is often on sustainable resource development—in other words, extracting resources at a lower rate than they are produced to ensure that the potential stock of natural resources is never fully depleted.

Whether the raw materials used in your industry are renewable or non-renewable will have a major impact on the way resources are managed. Renewable resources include things that are grown, like trees and produce, and also things that are raised, such as livestock; it also includes the harnessing of natural geological processes (rainwater, solar energy, wind power, hydro-electric or geothermic power, etc.). Non-renewable resources, on the other hand, either exists in limited amounts or require so much time to develop that they can be considered to exist in limited amounts. Minerals and petroleum are prime examples of non-renewable resources. If demand increases for a renewable resource, the supply can often be increased to meet it, though the process to do so may be cumbersome and time-intensive. When demand increases for a non-renewable resource, however, it almost invariably will translate to increased prices. New sources of the resource can be located, but no new resources can be created—in other words, the supply cannot be increased to meet the demand, creating an imbalance that must be carefully monitored by those managing the supply change.

The question of who owns the resource in question will also have an impact on how it factors into your supply chain. A national government controls resources that are state-owned; businesses will have little to no control over the cost or availability of state-owned resources. As the state ownership limits potential competition, prices for these resources will often be set, with few fluctuations. Resources that are privately owned, on the other hand, may offer several options to the business owner regarding pricing, quantity, and quality. These resources may be owned by an individual or a company, and though they are still potentially controlled somewhat by government regulations, the individual owner has more freedom to change the way they manage or sell their product, making competition more of a factor.

Location or development of new resources

As with general resource management, this can take on different forms depending on whether you are dealing with a renewable or a non-renewable resource. Even in the case of resources owned privately, the regulations of the local, state, or national government will have a significant impact on this stage of the supply chain, just as it does on the management of resources mentioned above.

When demand increases for a renewable resource, the response is often to make more of said resource available. The acquisition of more land is almost always required to accomplish this. The specific resource being developed will determine where these new resources will be created and what kind of land is required to produce them. Crops, for example, will need land that has rich soil and the correct seasonal weather to grow the crop in question properly. Occasionally, this also means the development or shaping of the land to suit the crop that will be grown on it.

In the case of alternative energy resources, this involves not only the acquisition of new land suitable for the purpose but also the construction and placement of the mechanisms required to capture said energy (a dam, wind turbines, solar panels, etc.). As with the land acquired for new crops, the key is to identify the land that will provide the maximum resource output with the lowest possible investment of both money and labor. It is far more likely in these industries for the land to be leased rather than purchased outright; multi-use arrangements are also fairly common, whether that means wind turbines built between crops in a farmer's field or hydro-electric dams utilized both for energy development and creation of new fishing areas. The manager of a supply chain looking to utilize these resources has to take the relative cost of construction and ongoing costs of land use into consideration when deciding which provider to use.

Increased efficiency in existing land is the other alternative to generating more resources to meet rising demand. Research into better crop rotation practices may be in order; new fertilizers and pesticides can be utilized to increase crop yields. In this case, the cost-benefit analysis will be focused on the time and labor involved to develop and implement these new technologies, products, or processes. The question that arises is whether the initial investment of time and money will generate a significant enough increase in resource production to pay ultimately off for everyone involved. The supply chain manager will need to convince the companies or individuals responsible for the resources involved that it is in their best interest to make the necessary changes; financial incentives from further downstream on the supply chain are often required to make this happen.

With non-renewable resources, exploration—or the location of new sources of resources—is going to be the focus at this stage of the supply chain. In the petroleum industry, for example, this takes the form of looking for untapped reserves both underground and underwater. Once those reserves are located, the same cost-benefit analysis has to be applied—in other words, whether the net total of new oil or natural gas that can be extracted from this untapped area will ultimately provide enough returns to justify the initial costs involved with setting up a new rig and drilling a new well.

Finding new sources of natural resources may change the way that resources factors into the supply chain. Continuing to use the oil industry as an example, the discovery of new on-shore oil reserves has forced many companies that rely on petroleum products to alter how they approach to supply chain management. These on-shore wells have a shorter drilling cycle than off-shore reserves. This translates into higher transaction volumes and a more flexible production schedule, and has shifted the balance from traditional purchase order processes to more standing contract agreements between petroleum extraction companies and their customers.

The question of relative cost based on resource availability also plays a role in whether companies that control natural resources decide to pursue exploration or development of new sources. The location of more on-shore drilling sites increased the availability of oil on the global market in the last few years. Because of this, the per-barrel price of oil has dropped significantly. This, too, has to be factored into any cost-benefit analysis. While drilling a new well will certainly increase a company's maximum yield, it may also devalue their entire supply to the point that drilling a new well becomes a negative value proposition. As with changes to how renewable resources are developed, a financial incentive from further downstream may be necessary to convince companies that producing more resources is in their best interest.

Resource collection

As with the above stages, this step on the supply chain will differ depending on the type of resource being collected. When it comes to crops, the harvesting of resources will be cyclical. Companies that utilize those resources will need to be aware when new crops become available to them, especially in cases where the harvest is seasonal. The cost of the resource may fluctuate throughout the year depending on average availability and the growing season of that particular item. Effectively managing the supply chain means being aware of the resource's peak production times to try and get the best possible per unit price. These peak production times will likely vary region by region, further complicating the cost-benefit model by making transportation costs part of the equation.

In the case of underground or underwater resources—such as oil, minerals, and metals—the collection stage involves bringing those resources to the surface through mines or wells. The availability of resources, in this case, will be more constant and less prone to seasonal fluctuations. When changes do happen, however, they will often be less predictable. The exhaustion of a previously well-producing mine could cause a major disruption to the supply and availability of the raw material. Staying abreast of these potential sweeping changes and making purchase decisions accordingly is one of the most important aspects of managing the supply chain at this stage.

Transportation

The transportation of raw materials to the factories that will process them is sometimes referred to as a midstream process because it serves as the transition between the upstream and downstream portions of the supply chain. Transportation costs and timing can have a major impact on the upstream stages of the supply chain, especially for companies that source their resources globally rather than regionally or locally.

The transportation of resources in the upstream stage includes any means by which raw materials are sent from the site of harvesting or extraction to the factories that will use or process the materials. This most often takes the form of freight by rail, road, sea, or air; it also includes things like pipeline networks that move crude oil from drilling sites to refineries. The manager of the supply chain should be aware of the relative cost of different methods of transportation and should factor that into purchasing decisions. As an example, a textiles company in the United States may find that cotton grown in Brazil is selling at a lower price than that grown in Georgia. Once the cost of the additional freight is factored into the equation, however, the ultimate cost of the Georgia cotton to the company may still be lower, making it the superior option despite its higher price point. Effectively managing the supply chain at this stage may mean staying abreast of trends in industries seemingly unrelated to the product at hand; the most obvious example of this would be fluctuations in the cost of fuel.

Storage of raw materials is also part of this stage. There are multiple points in the supply chain where this storage may take place. Producers of raw materials may have on-site storage facilities to help them maintain stock to meet customer demands. Factories that process those raw materials may also find it worthwhile to maintain warehouses or other storage facilities, especially if the availability or cost of the resource fluctuates widely between seasons. Buying larger quantities when prices are low and storing them on-site could ultimately prove more cost effective than buying as you go—especially in industries where the raw materials are not always consistently available.

Storage is also often handled through third-party providers. This can often be the most economical way to handle the transportation of raw materials to sites of production that are multiple regions or countries. Managing one warehouse could be a reasonable expense for your company, but managing multiple warehouses could be more of a headache than its worth. This is especially true in industries with special storage requirements for their raw materials, like certain pharmaceuticals in which the ingredients need to be kept refrigerated.

Challenges in upstream SCM

Environmental considerations are often a factor in upstream stages of the supply chain. While advancements in mining and drilling technology have reduced the impact of mineral and petroleum extraction on the environment, there is not yet a completely non-intrusive means of taking these resources out of the earth. Incidents like the Deepwater Horizon oil spill in April of 2010 have brought the environmental impact of underwater petroleum extraction back into the forefront. More recently, the potential environmental implications of fracking as a means of oil and gas extraction have been hotly contested. Fracking is thought to cause a wide array of environmental issues, from ground water contamination to earthquakes.

Though mining and drilling are the natural resource collection methods most often thought of as having environmental implications, other natural resources are not exempt from having issues. Deforestation due to the harvesting of lumber is a continuing problem throughout wooded areas of the world. The use of chemical pesticides and fertilizers to improve the yield of crops has also come under fire; these chemicals harm animals that accidentally consume them and are known to run off into rivers, causing unhealthy algae blooms and impacting the ecosystem. Keeping abreast of changing environmental regulations and the resulting changes in the cost and availability of raw materials are necessary for successful upstream supply chain management.

Because natural resources are just that—largely existing in an outdoor environment—they can also fall victim to natural, uncontrollable disasters. The impact of the forest fires that raged in Alberta, Canada during the spring of 2016 is one prime example. The oil pipelines running through this area of Canada were un-usable until the intensity of the fires waned, cutting off the supply of petroleum from wells in Alaska and northern Canada; the worldwide price of oil rose significantly as a result. Weather patterns and natural disasters that, on the surface, don't seem to have anything to do with the resource in question can still impact its availability. Identifying these potential issues—and being flexible enough to adapt to the changes in the market—is key to optimizing the upstream supply chain.

A variety of industries will often utilize companies that deal in raw materials. Because of that, their goals may or may not align with those of your specific company; rectifying those disparate goals in the context of your supply chain is important to maximizing your efficiency. Unfortunately, this also gives these resource developers a large amount of autonomy, which can often translate into a lack of visibility into their inner operations. This asset control can make it hard for supply chain organizations to see things like the company's third-party spending, which can limit your ability to improve the efficiency of upstream processes. Differing standards and practices from region to region can also be a major hurdle for those supply chain companies who work with organizations all around the world.

Chapter 4:
Downstream Processes

Downstream processes in the supply chain start with the manufacturing of products and go the whole way through their distribution to the customers. This may be a direct two-step process in more simple supply chains, or it could have multiple stops along the way, including the production of parts, the assembly of those into finished products, and the distribution of those products to warehouses and retail outlets. The marketing and sales aspects of business are also located on the downstream side of things, which includes identifying customer needs and points of high demand through analysis of sales data, as well as generating sales through advertising and customer interaction. Post-sale support is another overlooked aspect of supply chain management—who will handle returns, ensure customer satisfaction, and, when applicable, technical support. The closer a company or function is to the final consumer, the further downstream the process is considered to be, though not all companies on the downstream side of the supply chain have direct contact with customers.

Compared to the upstream side of the supply chain, third-party providers are more likely to be utilized on the downstream side of things. Considering the complexity of processes involved in the downstream side of this, this is hardly surprising. This is most likely to be the case on logistical matters, including transportation, storage, and customer distribution. Marketing and advertising can frequently be outsourced to specialists. The analysis of sales data and forecasting of future trends is also an area where companies are likely to seek outside help; some third-party agencies specialize in one of these particular aspects while others provide more over-arching support.

Product development and innovation is likely to be a major aspect of the downstream side of supply management, especially in technical, timely, and trendy businesses. Companies whose primary mode of sale is through catalogs may flip over fifty percent or more of their stock between mailings, necessitating a quick turnaround on the development of new ideas. Businesses whose stocks change on a seasonal basis—the fashion industry is a prime example of this—will also need to put a more significant amount of their energy into the development of new products. The ability of these businesses to stay on top of, or even ahead of, incoming trends will be one major factor in their ability to compete in the global market.

Production

There are many individual steps along a given supply chain that can be considered part of the production stage; the complexity of the product being constructed will largely determine how many steps are included upon its particular supply chain at this stage. Even seemingly simple products may have several different factories involved in the production process. A factory that makes clothes may work with a factory that weaves raw cotton into textiles, another one that makes buttons, and still another that makes zippers, and so on—but even the zipper manufacturers will work with a metal working facility that creates the teeth, someone else who makes the thread, still another for plastic components, and so on. At each of these stages in the process, the company that makes the item in question will be looking to maximize their profits, meaning their interests may or may not be in alignment with those of the steps further up the chain.

The further downstream a particular factory is, the more specific its production will be and the more interaction it will be likely to have with the end consumer. More generalized centers of production that work directly with raw materials and turn them into usable products—sheet metal manufacturers. For example, or petroleum refineries—are more likely to play a role in multiple supply chains, or even at different points along the same supply chain, which can make it more difficult for supply change managers to influence their policy or production decisions.

From a supply chain perspective, the production stage is critical to maximizing the efficiency of the overall chain. It is where processes will vary the most between industries, and also where the quality of the final product will be determined. Beyond that, there are innumerable decisions that must be made at a logistics level that will play a huge role in the financial success or failure of the final product. Different supply models will suggest having different levels of material or component inventories. The effective supply chain manager will strike a balance between keeping the on-hand inventory as low as possible to reduce waste and keeping enough to cope with changes to the level of demand. Accurate forecasting of trends, as noted in chapter 2, is imperative to ensure the shortest possible customer lead times with the minimum possible leftover stock at the end of the season. Other considerations at the production level include determining which aspects of production to do in-house and which should be outsourced to dedicated third parties, the relative size and timing of production runs to make the correct amount of product with maximum efficiency, and an awareness of current market fluctuations in upstream processes to keep material costs as low as possible.

Distribution

The distribution stage of the supply chain encompasses everything that goes into getting the product from the factory to the end consumer, including storage of inventory, freight and shipping routes, order fulfillment, and the monitoring of stock at retail outlets. Depending on the industry, distribution can take some forms. A company that makes metal fasteners may deal primarily with bulk orders from other factories and manufacturers; their distribution needs will be very different from those of the fashion industry example used above, who may distribute products mainly to retail stores but still operates off a model with an individual customer as the end consumer.

Perishable products that require specialized storage will present the biggest challenge to supply chain managers at this stage of the process. This includes (but is not limited to) food items like dairy and meat products as well as certain medicines produced by pharmaceutical companies, such as insulin. These sorts of industries will have the additional expenditure of refrigerated or climate-controlled freight and storage, and will need to be more sensitive to the timeliness of customer deliveries to minimize waste. For these companies, a more limited, regional distribution model may be the best option; alternatively, the utilization of third-party distribution companies with a specialization in perishable freight could be the most efficient choice.

Efficiency is ultimately the name of the game when it comes to distribution. Aside from the special circumstances noted above, the best distribution method is the one that gets the product to the customer the fastest and with the lowest possible cost. Distribution is one of the most common aspects of the supply chain to be outsourced, especially when it comes to the global marketplace. It is also the place where international regulations—like customs clearances and tariffs—can come into play, one of the other reasons global distribution is so frequently sent to third-party companies that are familiar with the intricacies of international trade.

Even if you don't use a third-party company for distribution in your main sales network, being partnered with someone who can provide those services over the extended sales area can be one way to ensure customers who are geographically distant from the production site still receive their orders in a timely fashion and without unnecessary expense to the company. This removes many issues from the shoulders of the company's supply chain management department. While changes to shipping and fuel costs will still need to be addressed on the upstream side of things, those shipments will often be consistent and in large quantities, making the per-unit expenditure a reasonable one. Fulfilling customer orders in a wide sales network can sometimes mean shipping a single finished product to each of ten different locations, preventing you from lowering the per-unit cost as you do on the supply end. A third-party distributor working with many companies at once will still be able to make those bulk shipping orders, lowering the per-unit cost for everyone in their customer network.

Downstream processes in the internet age

The omnichannel supply chain mentioned in chapter 1 comes into play in the downstream end of the supply chain more so than in the upstream processes. Making the sales platform available online means that anyone anywhere can buy your product—potentially great for upping sales and revenue, but a fact that opens up its potential issues. Having a solid distribution method in place is key for this reason. Customers will often expect similarly short shipping and lead times, regardless of where they live in the world and how far that is from your production facilities—in many cases, they may not even be aware how far from the production facilities they are.

Interactivity is one of the main things that's changed on the downstream side of the process in the internet age. There are both positive and potentially challenging aspects to this. On the one hand, real-time interaction with customers lets you more accurately assess their response to products. Before, sales numbers were a company's main way of telling if a product was successful or not, and while that can still be a major indication, you can now also talk to customers and find out what exactly they liked and didn't like about the given product, possibly letting you make changes accordingly in future production runs.

On the other side of this equation, increased customer interactivity can raise the expectation for customized attention and products in the mind of consumers. Many in the modern era have come to expect that they'll get what they want, when they want it—and a decrease in brand loyalty over the past generation means they will not hesitate to go elsewhere to get it. This places a new kind of pressure on those who design and make products, and some might say allows the customer to have too much control and influence over the production process.

Many companies do offer customizable options on their products through their web sales platform. The feasibility of this from a supply chain perspective will greatly depend on what industry is being discussed and what manner of customization is taking place. If it is aesthetic—different colored exteriors for a computer, for example—production runs can still largely take place in bulk, with the customized aspects added immediately before shipping, thus preventing an increase in lead times or a reduction in efficiency. If more integral customization is to be offered, the emphasis should be shifted to producing larger runs of individual components that can be quickly assembled to order. Many computers and tech device companies take this approach to consumer customization. Generally speaking, the higher the profit margins on the product being made, the more practical this kind of customization will be.

Communication on the post-sale side has also changed with the rising global availability of the internet. Again, there are two sides to this coil. On the one hand, it can often be easier to offer post-sale support, whether that is through a dedicated support call center or live chat functions on the company's website. The ability to expand support can increase customer satisfaction and help to encourage repeat business. On the other hand, the modern consumer believes it is within their rights to return a product they are not one hundred percent satisfied with, and will often expect the company to foot the bill for shipping. Coping with these post-sale challenges can be especially difficult for smaller companies with relatively limited staff and profit margins.

Challenges in downstream SCM

As both the potential customer base and the potential competition are increased through globalization, product design is increasingly expected to drive demand. Building a quality product is sometimes no longer enough to bring people to your product; being aware of the products offered by the competition and making your product different—then convincing customers those extra features are necessary for them—is increasingly necessary to stay competitive. For supply chain managers, this means staying current with industry news and developments and ensuring the production line is flexible enough to cater to potential changes in the needs of the end consumer.

While environmental concerns are often less of a factor on the downstream side of production, social and ethical concerns still come into play. The issue of workers' rights has been at the forefront of the global consciousness in recent years. Major companies have come under fire for using factories in less developed companies. While these facilities can often provide lower labor and production costs, concerns over poor conditions and inhumane treatment of workers may work against you with increasingly socially conscious customers. Depending on the product and the industry, customers may be willing to pay more for products they know been made in factories that provide a good work environment. Balancing low production costs with ethical considerations can present a major challenge for the modern company.

Chapter 5:
Integrated Companies

An organization that combines both upstream and downstream aspects of the production is known as an integrated company. There are two broad categories of integration. In horizontal integration, one company produces several related components or products that exist at the same level of the supply chain. An example of this would be a factory that makes computers, tablets, and cellular phones from the same production equipment. Vertical integration, on the other hand, refers to an arrangement where one company owns multiple levels of the supply chain. In this arrangement, there will typically be multiple facilities owned by the company, each of which produces a different aspect of the finished product. An example of this would be a computer manufacturer that also owns the companies that make the circuit boards and housing (as opposed to purchasing components from an outside supplier).

In certain industries, integration may occur naturally or be the standard for the industry. One prominent example of this would be a traditional dairy farm. The farm controls the production of raw material (the cows) and oversees the extraction of those materials (the milking apparatus). While they may ship the milk to outside companies to make products like yogurt and butter, very often the pasteurization and bottling of the milk are done right there, on the farm. In this way, the development, extraction, and processing of the resource all take place within the same facility. Customers may even be able to come to the farm and buy their milk directly; restaurants often source their milk directly from a farm, meaning even the distribution side of the process is handled in-house.

Situations like the one described above perfectly illustrate the idea of integration but are not especially common in industries outside of food production. In most cases, integration is only accomplished through careful planning and acquisition of outside facilities, rather than occurring naturally within the industry. While integration can certainly maximize a company's efficiency, it is also incredibly difficult to implement successfully, and potentially disastrous when it fails.

Vertical integration

Vertical integration is one means by which modern companies can prevent the hold-up problem. This issue arises when two companies could maximize their efficiency through communication and cooperation but are hesitant to do so out of self-interest—one or both is concerned that cooperation will decrease their bargaining power and ultimate profits. When both companies are under the same ownership umbrella, cooperation is assumed, and maximum efficiency is ultimately possible.

Vertical integration is hardly a new concept. As early as the nineteenth century, steel industry magnate Andrew Carnegie practiced vertical integration in his companies. He controlled both the iron ore and coal mines where he sourced raw materials, the coke ovens that cooked the coal, and the mills where steel was made. In Carnegie's hands, this integration led to what is known as a vertical monopoly—a situation in which, by controlling the means of production along the entire supply chain, competing companies either cannot get access to necessary steps along the supply chain or cannot do so at the same low price point, thus rendering them ineffective in the competitive marketplace.

There are three broad types of vertical integration, depending on which direction the integration is moving within the supply chain. A backward vertical integration goes further upstream than the company in question. In other words, the company takes control of some of the subsidiaries that make the components ultimately used to build the product. An example of this would be a car company that takes ownership of the glass factory that makes the windshields, the sheet metal factory that makes the car frame and body, and so on. A forward vertical integration looks further downstream toward the means of distribution. This would involve purchasing retail centers, or perhaps buying a fleet of trucks that are responsible for product distribution. When the integration goes both upstream and downstream, it is called balanced integration.

There are several prominent examples of integrated companies in the modern commercial landscape. One of the most well-known (and most successful) is the Apple computer company, which has used a vertical integration technique for over three decades. Apple integrates software production with hardware production across devices, letting them control the entire process from start to finish. They also own their retail and distribution centers which handle both initial sales and post-sale support. While Apple does outsource some stages of the production process (notably assembly) the fact that they control a large swath of their supply chain lets them stay competitively priced, and also allows them to make quicker decisions as to product design changes. Other companies that have successfully utilized vertical integration ExxonMobil, Bell, and 20th Century Fox.

One theme you may be noticing in the companies that have successfully utilized vertical integration is their size. Generally speaking, the smaller the company, the more difficult and risky vertical integration becomes. This is one of the factors that has led policymakers to turn a wary eye on vertical integration because it makes competition within the marketplace exceptionally difficult. This most notably happened within the media industry, when the Supreme Court was called to rule in a case against Paramount Pictures that called for five of the largest motion picture companies to sell their theaters, limiting the industry's vertical integration.

Pros and cons of vertical integration

There are many potential advantages to a vertically integrated company. The centralization of the supply chain's control makes the process vastly more efficient, allowing companies better to meet the sometimes conflicting demands of customer intimacy and product development. Companies that utilize vertical integration have an average of 45 fewer full-time supply chain employees than those that use traditional models. By increasing the efficiency, this allows the companies to offer a better price to the end consumer without diminishing profit margins. The company can control where its raw materials come from and how they are utilized, and can prevent potential delays caused by increased demand. This is especially important when the industry works with materials that are rare or tend to vary widely in price throughout the year.

Vertical integration allows a company to synchronize supply with demand throughout the production process. This significantly lowers uncertainty in the production process and can translate to a lessened need to maintain an inventory of raw materials and components—when you control the means of producing components, you do not have to worry whether that factory will be able to adapt to peaks in demand.

Obviously, any system with such high potential payoffs comes with associated high degrees of risk. The larger the overall organization becomes, the more difficult it is to make changes to either the suppliers or the buyers of the finished products. The upstream side of an integrated supply chain may also suffer in quality as a result. With a guaranteed buyer in place for the components and materials produced, the motivation to innovate and to produce high-quality products is potentially diminished. A fully-integrated supply chain can also fall victim to an overly rigid organizational structure, making it less flexible and less adaptable to change.

From a social perspective, vertical integration encourages the creation of industry monopolies. While this can be an advantage for the company by limiting competition and increasing potential profit margins, that limited competition can also lead to higher end consumer costs. A monopoly also lessens the motivation to innovate new products or better products. Over time, this can backfire for a large, fully-integrated company. They may become gradually less sensitive to individual customer needs, allowing smaller companies to step in and take over in certain markets. Because of the size of their overall corporation, the vertically integrated company may be less able to adapt to this small competition as quickly as it needs to.

Chapter 6:
Effective Supply Chain Management

The definition of supply chain management depends on whom you are talking to and what kind of business you are in. Some see it as a concept with the primary objective of integrating and managing the sourcing of materials and their flow across the various businesses that work with them, ultimately creating a finished product. Others see it more from the customer end of the equation, as a way to extend the consumer's needs and requirements the entire way up and down the stream of production so that the goals of quality customer service, lower inventory, and reduced per unit cost can be balanced and met. In its simplest terms, supply chain management integrates the flow of the distribution channel from the primary supplier of raw materials all the way through the end user.

There are a few different theories and approaches to effective supply chain management. Some economic experts view it regarding a management philosophy or an implementation philosophy; others view it more practically, as a set of management processes. It can also be viewed in operational terms, as a flow of materials and products from one point in the supply chain to another. The way you view supply chain management in your particular business will largely depend on the challenges of your industry's specific processes.

When viewed as a philosophy, supply chain management views the supply chain as a single entity, as opposed to looking at the individual links on the chain that each performs their function. This philosophical look at the supply chain extends the idea of a partnership and makes the supply chain a multi-firm entity. The goal is to synchronize the intra-firm operational capabilities, converging the strategies of the disparate steps on the chain into one single goal.

Regardless of which definition or approach you use, supply chain management is less about a chain of businesses that interact one-on-one at each stage in the process and more about an interconnected network of businesses extending information and control forward and back so that every stage of the production is working toward the same ultimate goal. The sharing of information is one of the primary goals of this multidisciplinary collaboration. As the marketplace shifts to an increasingly more global and competitive model—and as the complexity of products in the modern marketplace increases—supply chain management becomes even more important to staying competitive. Product design and development are also increasingly more necessary to maintain a strong focus on as consumers have ever more options of which product in a given field they want to go with.

Supply chain management uses concepts that were developed in a variety of disciplines, including marketing, economics, operational management and research, and information systems. It is focused on all aspects of the process, from integrating and managing the sourcing and flow of raw materials through their various levels of customer. Synchronization of incoming materials with the orders from customers and the ultimate delivery of the final product lets you achieve both lower costs and better customer service when managed correctly.

Value propositions

One of the most important results of a well-managed supply chain is the ability of a company to increase the value proposition for the customers. When we talk about value propositions, we are referring to the benefits that the customers receive from using or purchasing your particular product over those of the competitors. This value proposition can come from any stage of the process whether it is the types of materials you use, the way the product is designed and constructed, or your method of transportation and delivery.

At the same time, the value is increased for the customer; companies need to think about how value is increased or decreased for the business as a result. Any activity that you perform in a business context will have associated costs; they key, from a supply chain management perspective, is to make sure those costs are exceeded by revenue, which translates into a higher profit margin for the business. While this may seem counterintuitive, effective and efficient management of the supply chain can simultaneously increase the value proposition for the customer and the ultimate profit margin of the company. The value chain or value network of your company looks at all of the activities that the organization carries out, dividing them into primary and secondary activities and assessing where value is highest and where it can be increased.

Adding value for the customer in the modern era can take many forms. Adding value for today's consumer means more than just making your product the way you always have. It is important to deliver something to the customer they cannot get anywhere else, either because they cannot carry out the same steps in the process or can't match the cost. When it comes to convincing a customer that you can provide them with a value proposition, you should show them that you perform activities they are unable or unwilling to do themselves, or that you have a product they are willing to pay for out of convenience or an increase in quality.

The value proposition of your company could come out of a variety of sources. It could be because of your advanced knowledge—that you have skills and information the customers do not have or can't access. It could be about accepting risks in production that the customer is unwilling to shoulder themselves. It could be due to your location compared to the customer if you operate in a region where the supplies are at a low price point while they are in a place that they are at a high price point. The economy of scale is often a part of a company's value proposition—by creating the items in a larger volume, you can more efficiently create a stock, therefore decreasing the per-unit cost for your customer who would not be able to replicate that cost on a smaller scale.

Whatever the source of your value proposition, it should be in keeping with your company's overall identity and strategy. Identifying what value your particular company adds to the product for the customer is an important step in choosing your method of supply chain management; altering your management approach to suit the best value proposition is often more effective than the opposite approach of looking for value in the way you run you company. In every situation, value networks acknowledge that companies rarely stand alone, and relies on all the parties in the chain working well together.

Inventory

Storage and levels of inventory can be one of the most challenging aspects of supply chain management, especially if you are in an industry with significant variation in demand depending on the season. Effective management allows you to minimize backstock of inventory, reducing waste while still maintaining (or even improving) your level of customer service. Proper synchronization lets you react quickly to changes in the market or shifts in order sizes.

The traditional model of inventory management is that seen in supermarkets and other retail stores. In these situations, the company that produces the goods rarely interacts directly with the customer; instead, retail outlets have a certain amount of inventory on hand, which they replenish through an order to the supplier once it falls below a designated level. This can mean fairly large orders arriving without much notice at the suppliers, forcing the production stages of the supply chain to be constantly ready to provide more inventory at the drop of the hat. Ultimately, this can be a waste of labor time and sometimes of supplies, depending on the nature of your industry. A more efficient model is to integrate the suppliers with the retail stores so that the suppliers have access to the inventory levels at the purchase point of the chain. This allows the production side of the supply chain to anticipate demand rather than waiting for the order to come in.

The life cycle of the product in question will have a significant impact on the inventory, as well. In cases where the products are stable on the shelf and have a long life cycle (items that are non-seasonal and non-perishable), it is often easier to manage inventory levels, and can sometimes be more efficient to maintain larger quantities of inventory on hand.

Where inventory management becomes especially important is in industries with a short life cycle or unstable shelf presence. In these cases, the excess stock can often become waste; a longer lead time for customers at points of peak demand is often preferable to the significant product waste that results from maintaining inventory backstock. In these cases, the supply chain manager should have his eye toward improving responsiveness to customer orders to cut down on that high lead time at peak demand points.

The level of customization involved in making the product also makes a difference at the inventory stage of the process. If products are relatively consistent across orders, building to stock is a faster and more efficient way to manage the inventory. On the other hand, products that are fully customizable and are often built to order cannot be constructed until the order arrives. In this case, the flexibility of the production side is key. Making components to par when possible is the best way to reduce lead time in order fulfillment and prevent backlogs in the production stage when demand increases.

Logistics and information technology

When to use third-party companies—and for what stages of the process—is also an important question for the effective supply chain manager to answer. Logistics companies are the most consistently utilized; storage and distribution costs can be significantly lessened by going with a company that has expertise in global distribution and maintains warehouses in a variety of global locations.

There are several choices you have to make on the logistical side of the equation from a supply chain perspective.

Who will transport your goods—the buyer, the seller, or a third-party company? The same question applies to storage as well. Will excess inventory mostly exist at the production level, at the retail level, or in an outside warehouse? Choosing the correct pathway for delivery to maximize responsiveness is an important consideration, as well. The question of quality assurance often arises as well. At what stage is that handled, and by whom? If the customer does not believe the quality is there and wants to return the product—or wants to return the product for another reason—how are those returns to be handled? All of these questions will arise in the course of constructing an ideal management plan for your supply chain.

When it comes to information technology, third-party companies are helpful in the downstream portion of the supply chain through what are known in the business world as the "six Is" of SCM: Intelligence, interactivity, integration, individualization, independence, and industry. Intelligence refers to the tracking of user activity and analysis of product sales and popularity, information which is sent along to warehouses and distributors. Interactivity refers to the customization of production by the customer. Integration involves the linking of suppliers to production and purchasing stages of the supply chain. Individualization is on the advertising side of things—customizing marketing to individual users to increase engagement. Independence means being un-tethered to location-based suppliers and distribution points through effective globalization efforts. The industry is all about the structure of the supply chain, organizing the stages better to create a more sophisticated order process and speed up the delivery of goods to the customer. Because these aspects are all inter-related and also fairly complex, it is becoming more and more common for the IT side of the supply chain equation to be outsourced to a third-party company, as well.

Challenges in supply chain management

The two main challenges with SCM are alignment and linkage. Alignment refers to the common vision and goal across all stops on the supply chain. Proper alignment means everyone is consistently working towards the same objectives, no matter where he or she are in the chain. Improper alignment leads to inefficiency, inconsistency, and potential conflicts of interest. Linkage refers to the sharing of information up and down the supply chain and the use of that information to make plans and decisions. It requires open, active avenues of communication between all those responsible for decision-making at all levels of the chain. Good linkage keeps everyone on the same page; poor communication, on the other hand, can have similar issues to poor alignment—lack of efficiency or consistency.

There is a concept referred to as the Bullwhip Effect that can also have an effect on supply chain management. This concept describes the way that small changes in demand at the customer level can be amplified as these orders pass up the supply chain, in much the same way the vertical movement in a cracked whip is broader the further you get from the tip. The consequences of the Bullwhip Effect can include fluctuation in inventory levels, either on the side of excess or shortage; it can also induce longer lead times and extra cost at the manufacturing and transportation levels, as well as potential damage to the relationship and trust between the partners within the supply chain. Improving the communication between the customer side of the supply chain and the previous levels can help prevent the deleterious consequences of the Bullwhip Effect.

The complexity of the supply chain will also have some influence over the difficulty of managing it, as well. There are three general categories of supply chain complexity: direct, extended, and ultimate. A direct supply chain consists of only three steps: the company, the supplier, and the customer. An extended supply chain is slightly more complex, including the suppliers of the suppliers and the customers of the customers—a chain most commonly seen in industries where the end user is more of a corporate entity than an individual. An ultimate supply chain is the most complex form, involving various chains of supply and demand across multiple industries and pathways. While a direct or an extended supply chain can often be managed easily without outside help, if you are part of an ultimate supply chain, third-party logistics providers will almost certainly be necessary.

There are many aspects and variations within individual supply chains. The geographical distance between stages in the supply chain, for example, will have an influence on the logistical issues, especially if the business spans multiple countries. Whatever the particular issues of your industry, managing the supply chain effectively involves paying close attention to market trends and ensuring open communication and coordination between various stops along the chain. It also involves taking a long-view of your industry. No matter how effective your particular node in the supply chain is, it will not matter if the rest of the industries you work with are inferior.

Conclusion

Supply chain management is an ever-evolving field of study. It only became a prominent topic in the field of economics in the 1980s. From a modern perspective, that was a long time ago—before the invention of the internet or the wide prominence of home computers. From a historical or academic perspective, however, that is not an especially long time, especially considering how much else has changed in the interim. The true complexities of supply chain management were only beginning to be understood when the introduction of commerce across the world wide web changed the way many people conduct business; as a result, the study of the field has evolved even as it is been explained, a unique situation for any economic concept.

The effective management of a supply chain has to do with far more than simply getting the best price from your suppliers or knowing how they'll be transported from point A to point B. It is an all-inclusive and forward-thinking concept aimed at maximizing efficiency at every level. For the purpose of study and discussion, the processes along the supply chain are divided into sections, whether those are the large-scale definitions of upstream versus downstream or the most compartmentalized definitions based on their section of the chain. While this makes it easier to discuss and analyze any issues along the supply chain, you can hopefully see after reading the preceding chapters that this does not mean they are truly separate processes. The optimized supply chain is a single entity from start to finish, each business or individual involved sharing the same goals and information profiting—or failing—as a unit.

There are many ways to run an effective supply chain. For some, integration is the best path to a higher profit margin; owning your suppliers or your means of distribution can increase your flexibility and control, allowing you to offer a better value proposition to your customers. For others, the opposite path may be the best option, outsourcing the aspects of your business that are too costly or time-intensive to handle on your own. Though there are guidelines and strategies that tend to work best in certain industries, what works for one company will not always work for another—and what worked for your company ten years ago may not be the best option now. Being flexible and open to new avenues is key to remaining competitive even through the changes that will naturally take place in your business as it grows.

Thank you

If you enjoy the book and bonus, please leave an Amazon review, it takes only 9 seconds :)

Your Bonus

Learn how to be a better leader, download your FREE BONUS at

http://successentrepreneur.org/supply-chain-management/

You may also schedule a FREE 30 min call with me to discuss the book or a related topic at

http://successentrepreneur.org/schedule-a-call/

My Other Books

The New Rich
http://www.amazon.com/gp/product/B01DGSJKT4

New Social Media Platforms in 2016
http://www.amazon.com/gp/product/B01EJ86IX6

Blogging for Beginners
http://www.amazon.com/gp/product/B01DR1IARI

You can also contact or follow me at:

www.SuccessEntrepreneur.org

Facebook: KhalidZidanOnline

Twitter: KhZidanOnline

44461592R00035

Made in the USA
San Bernardino, CA
15 January 2017